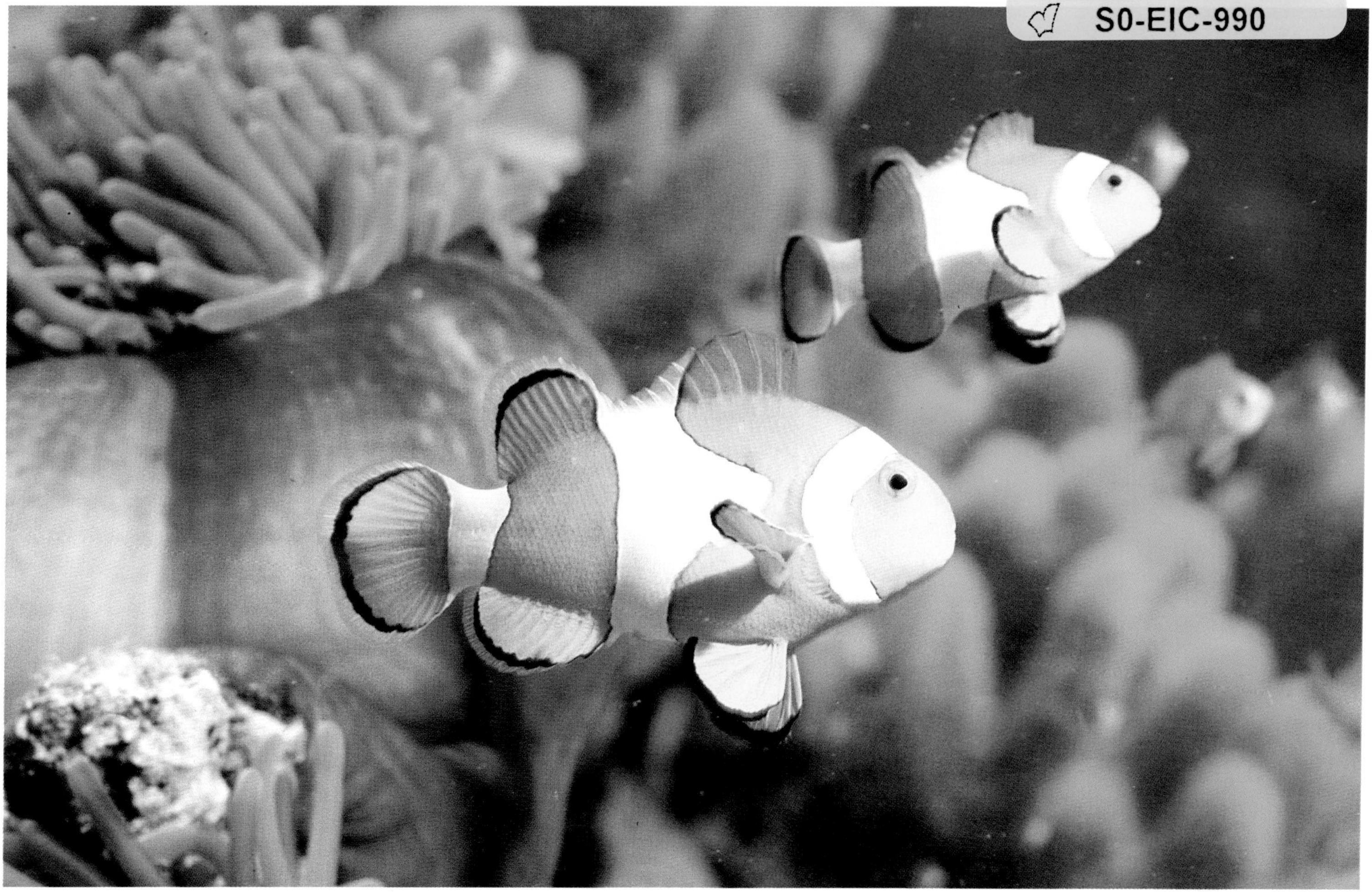

fish

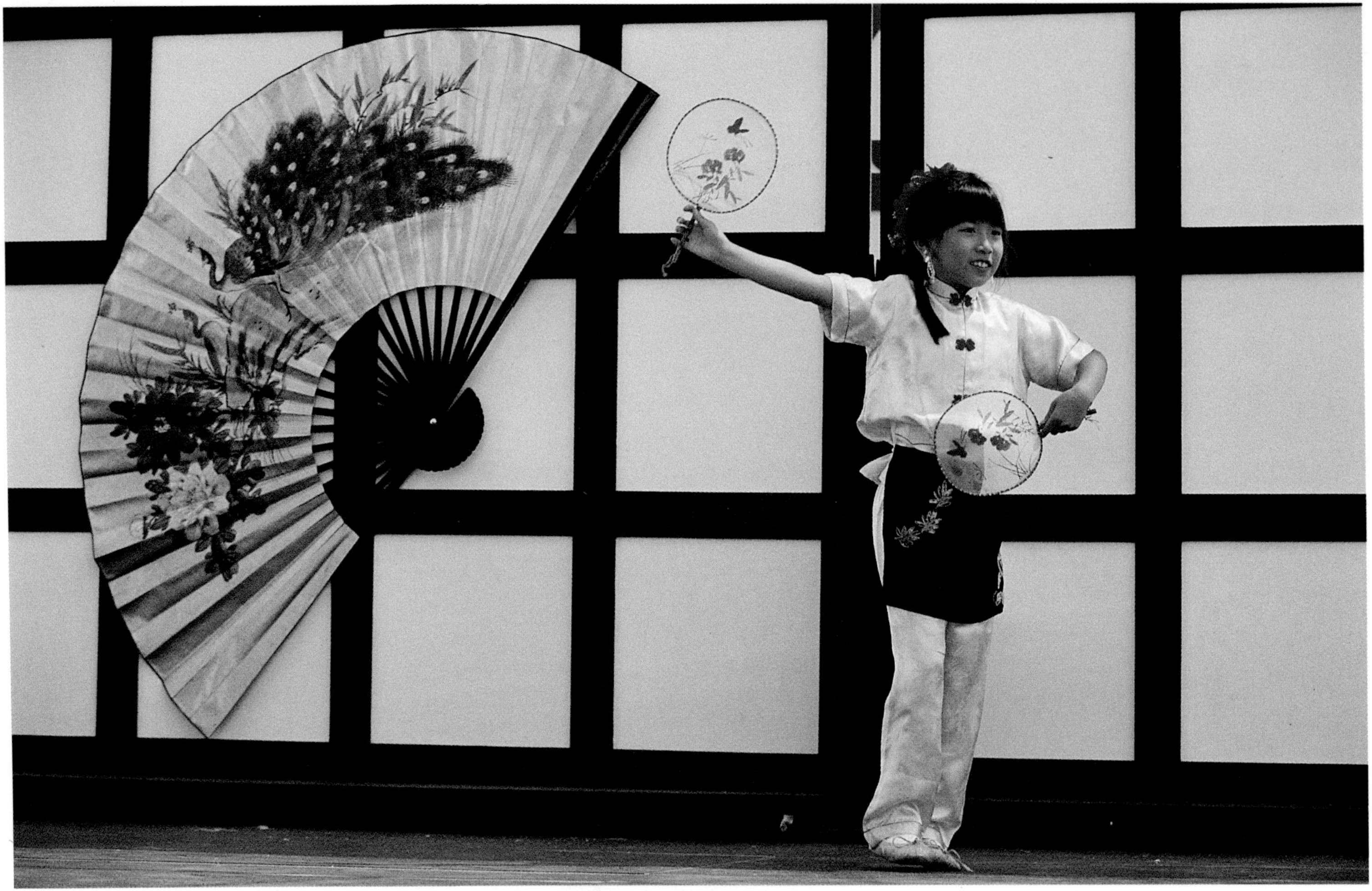

fans

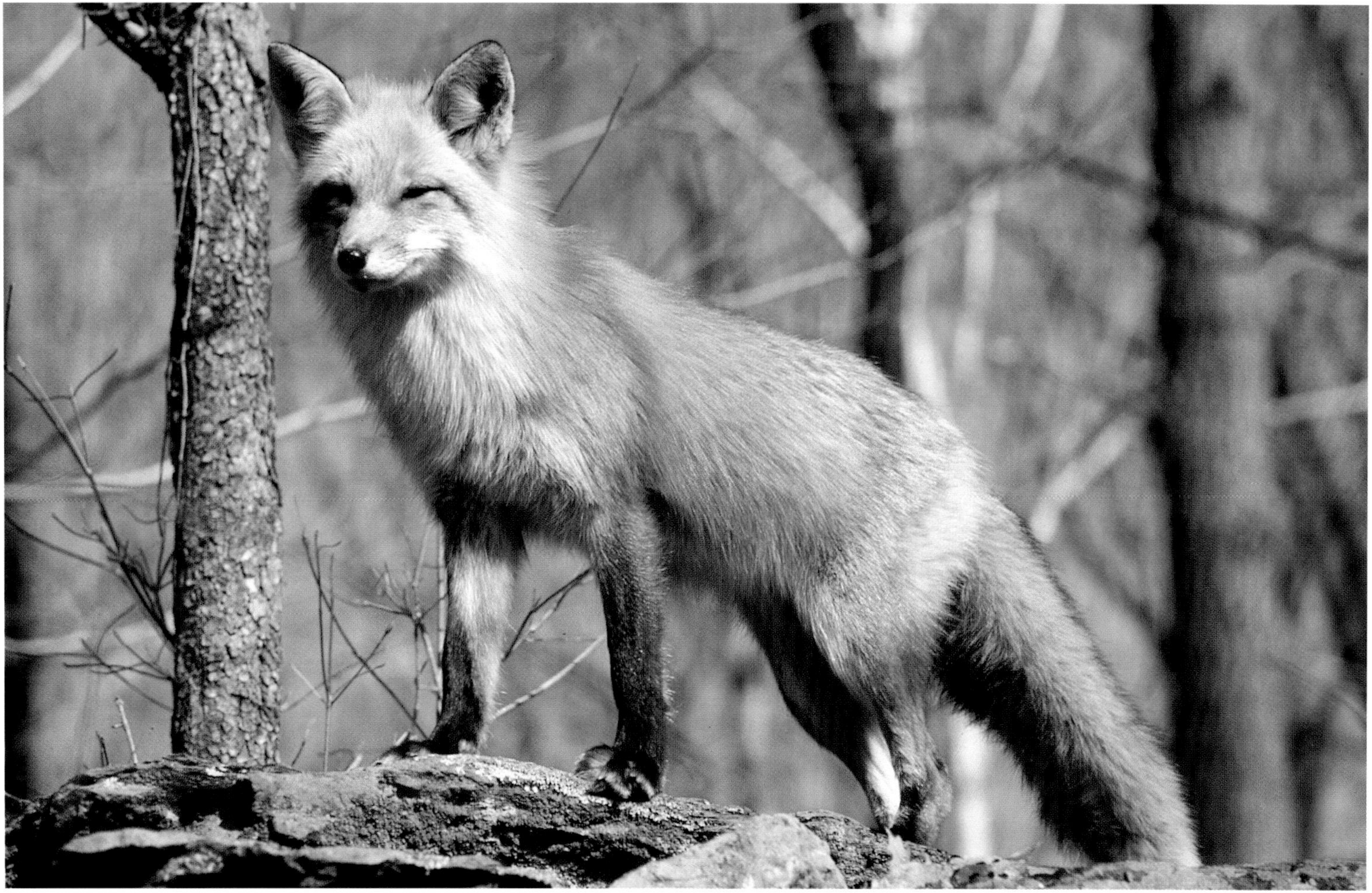

fox

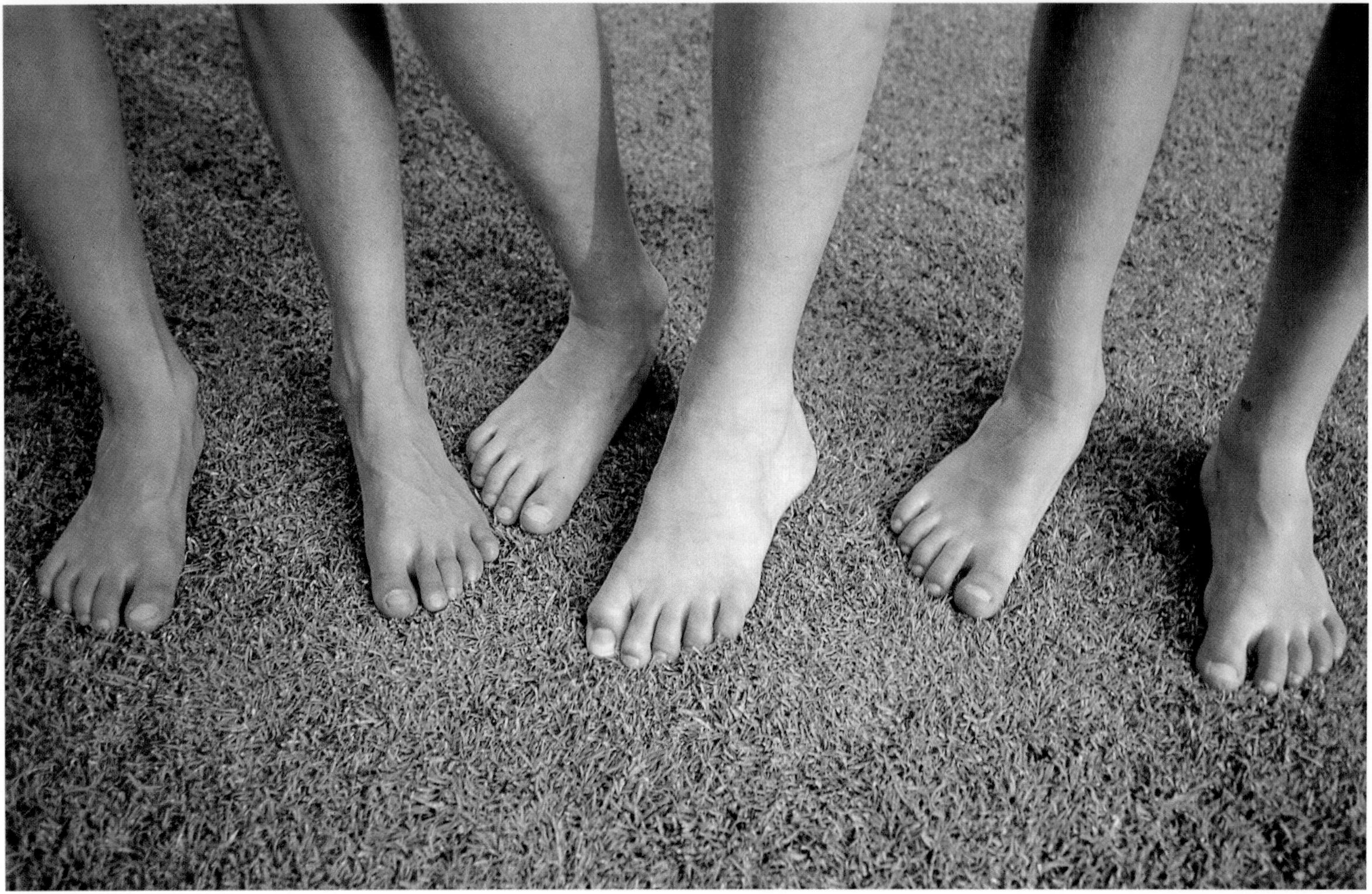

feet

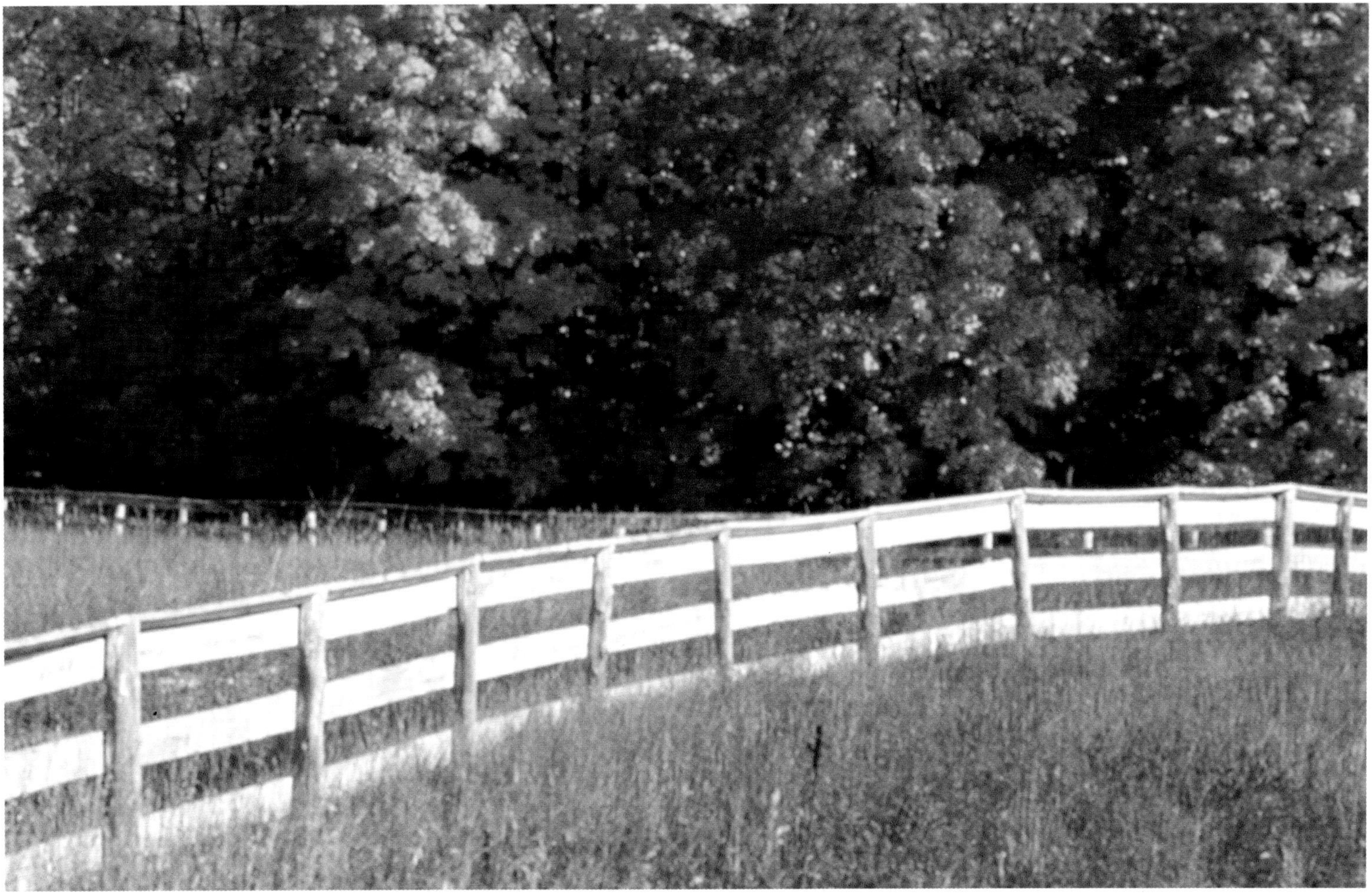

fence

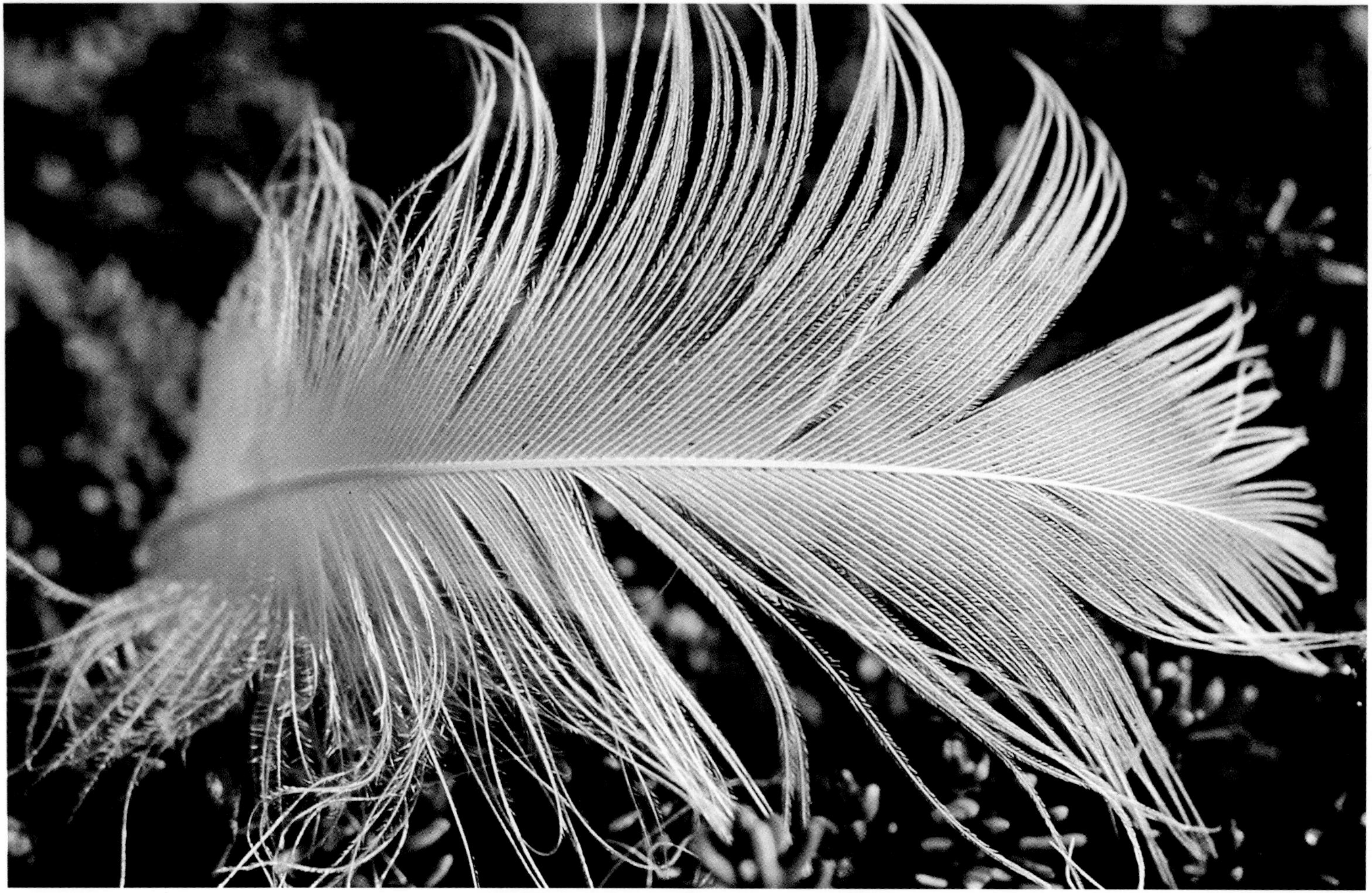

feather

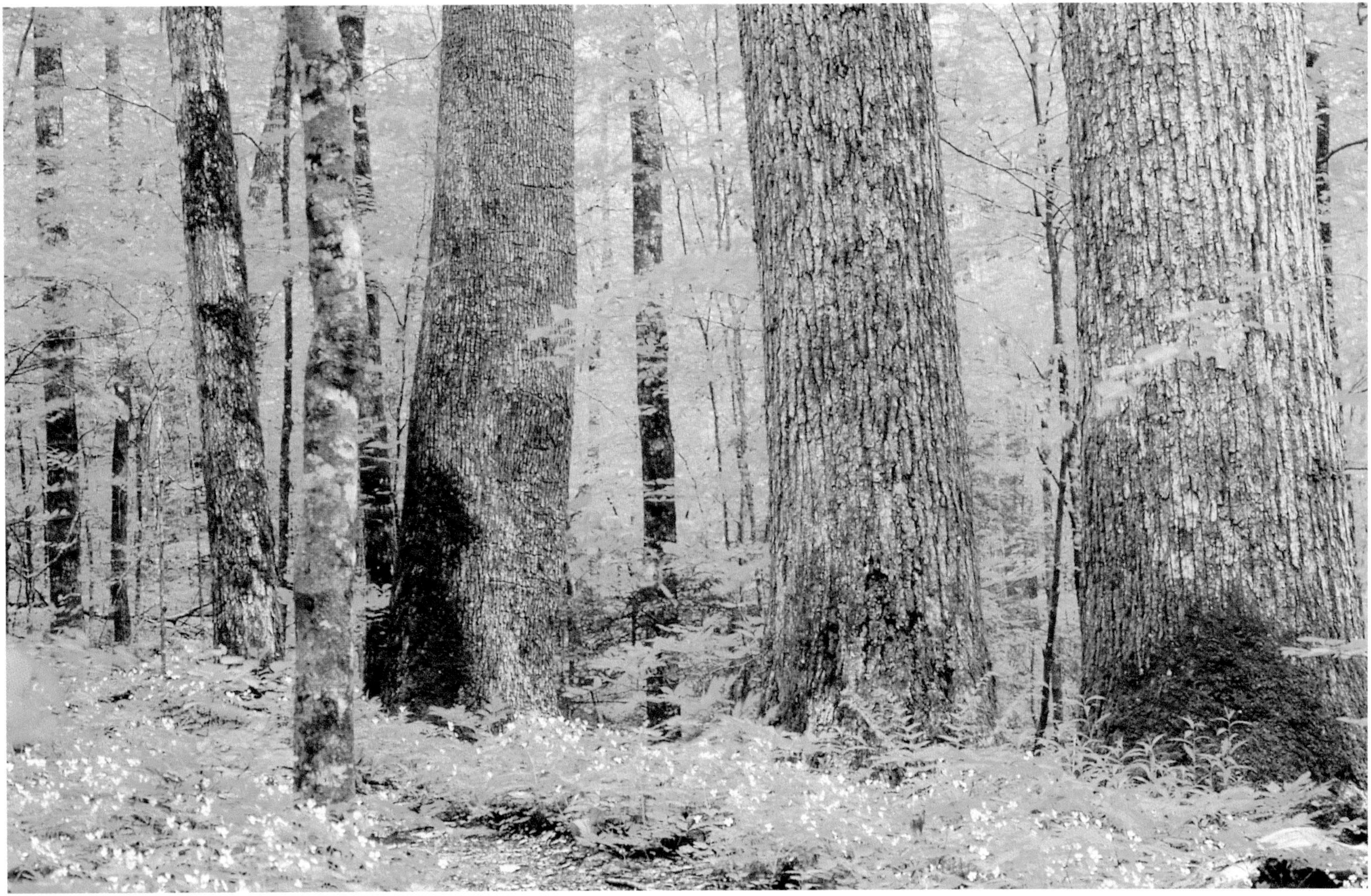

forest

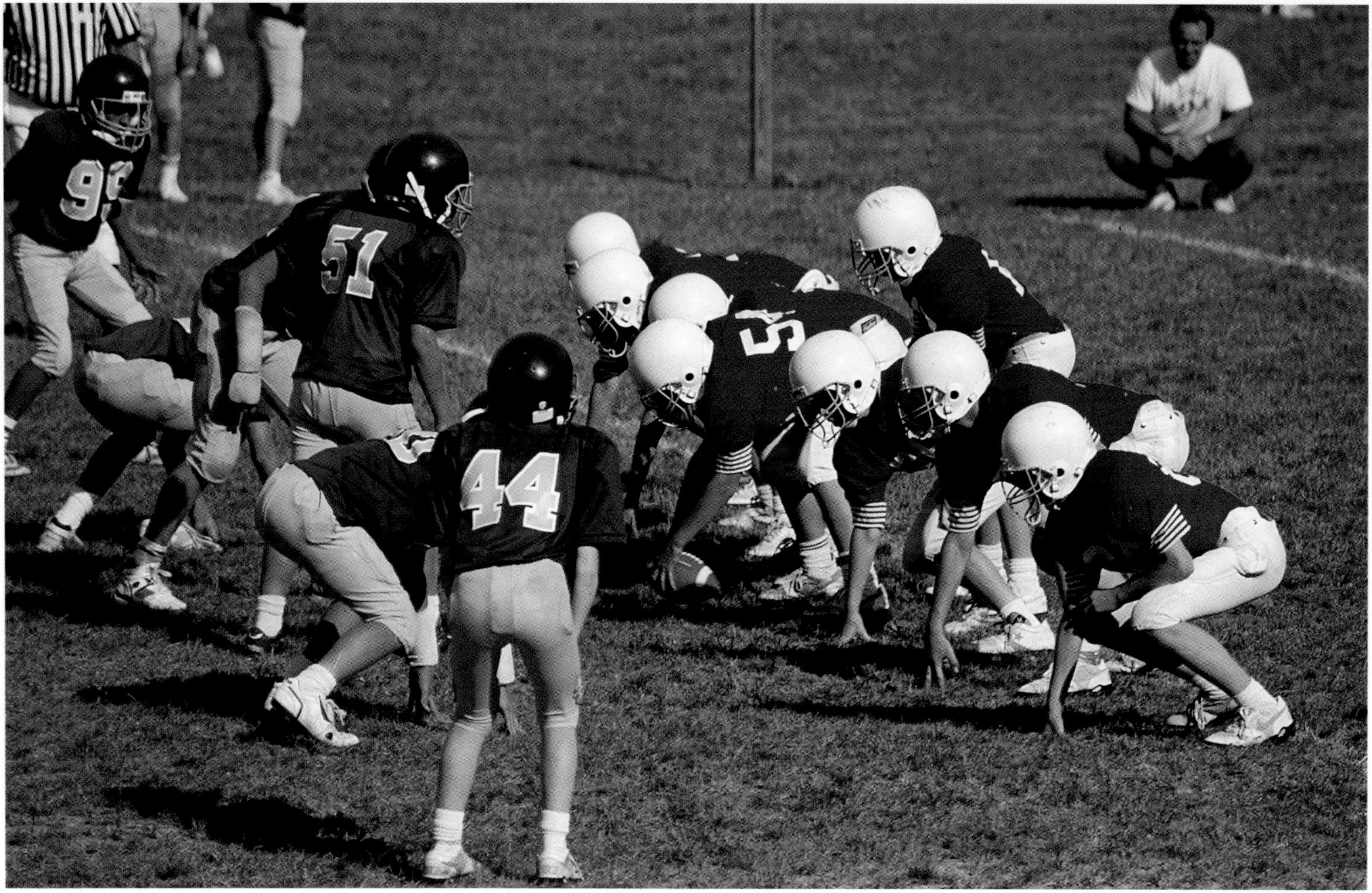

football